Disney·PIXAR Inside Out 2

Disney Animation Book

Disney · PIXAR

INSIDE OUT 2

Disney Animation Book

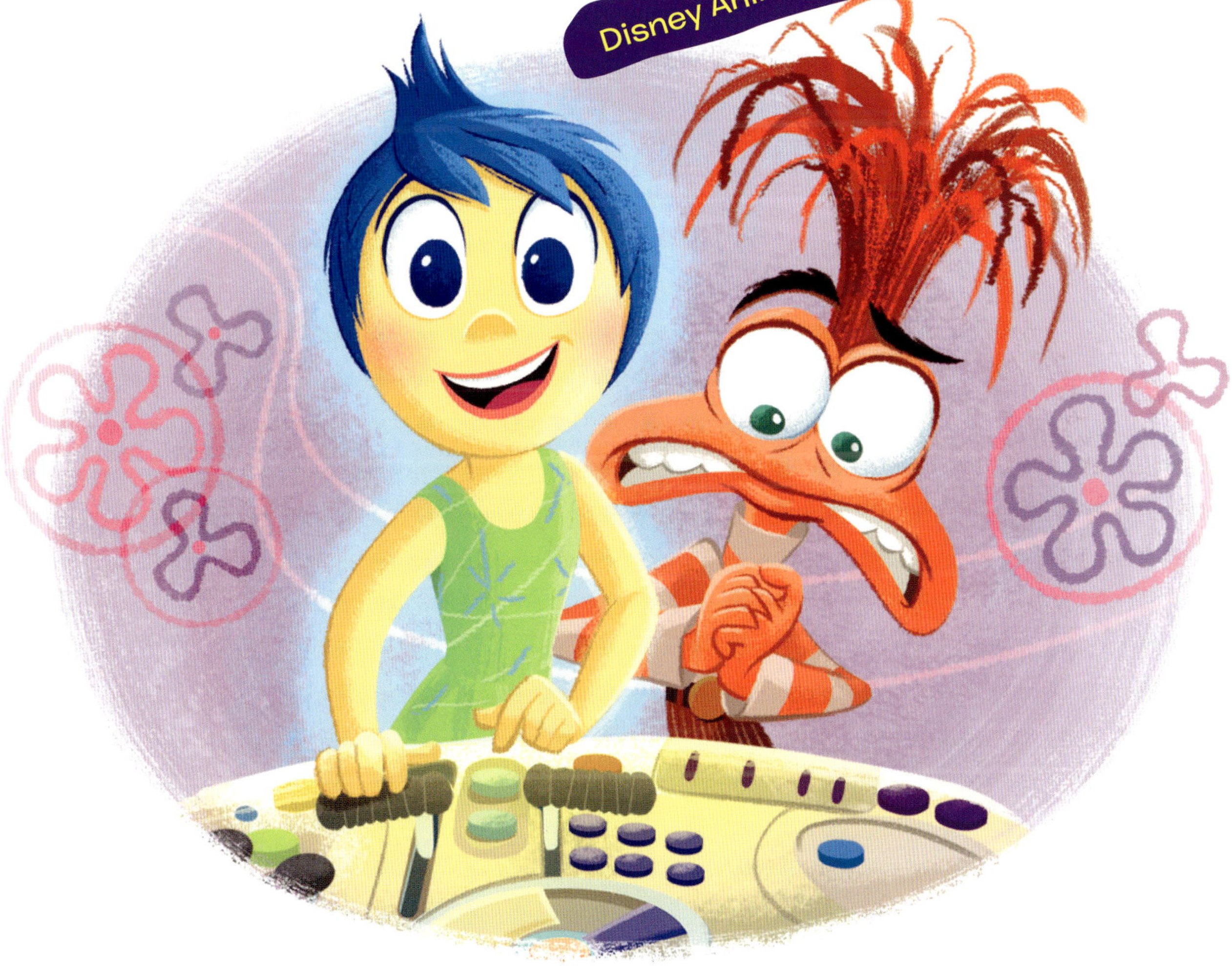

Adapted by
Cynthea Liu

Illustrated by
Alan Batson

Designed by
Tony Fejeran

Special thanks to Nick Balian

더모던
Themodern

MEET *the* CHARACTERS

RILEY

Riley is now thirteen and navigating all the ups and downs of being a teenager! Excited to attend hockey camp with her best friends, Bree and Grace, Riley hopes they will get a spot on the Fire Hawks team in school next year! But things take a turn when Riley finds out that she and her besties won't be going to the same school. . . .

JOY

Always a **CHEERFUL OPTIMIST,** Joy will do whatever it takes to make sure that her girl, Riley, has an awesome life. Working with fellow Emotions Anger, Disgust, Fear, and Sadness, Joy has her tried-and-true plans to keep Riley happy and protect her Sense of Self. But all that changes the day some new Emotions show up!

ANGER

Though he can be pretty hot-headed and **EXPLOSIVE,** Anger is willing to risk anything and take any chances, all to get the very best for Riley.

DISGUST

Now that Riley is a teenager, Disgust's role is even more important. Disgust is in charge of knowing what's **COOL** and what isn't, and she isn't afraid to point out when something is totally **CRINGE**.

FEAR

Fear may be **OVERPROTECTIVE** of Riley, but that's only because he's always terrified. Fear's job is to keep Riley as **SAFE** as he can, so he's always on the lookout for danger.
But Fear can't possibly be prepared for what happens when the new Emotions arrive.

SADNESS

Besides being pretty sad, Sadness is not very confident in herself, but Joy knows that Sadness **HAS WHAT IT TAKES** to help make Riley's life amazing. Constantly concerned that she might do something to ruin everything, Sadness must learn to overcome her self-doubt when the new Emotions appear!

MEET the CHARACTERS

ANXIETY

Anxiety is **NERVOUS** and worried, to say the least. Always thinking ten steps ahead, Anxiety has sworn to be prepared for every possible pitfall in Riley's life, to make sure she fits in with her peers and never makes a mistake . . . no matter what Anxiety has to do to make it happen.

EMBARRASSMENT

Embarrassment is **BIG**, **AWKWARD**, very **SHY**, and clumsy, but he has a big heart. While he can't turn invisible, Embarrassment does the next best thing to make himself feel less noticed: he pulls the drawstring on his hoodie tight, closing it around his face. It kind of works. . . .

ENVY

SMALL but **MIGHTY**, Envy helps Riley figure out what she wants. Unfortunately, Envy wants a lot and doesn't always appreciate what Riley already has! When Envy sets her sights on Riley becoming a part of the varsity hockey team, she won't let Riley's best friends, Bree and Grace, get in the way.

ENNUI

Ennui prefers to stay put on her couch in Headquarters. She's too **BORED** to get up, so she drives the console by using an app on her phone. Ennui doesn't care about anything, which is valuable to teenage Riley, who's trying to appear **COOL** to her friends.

Thirteen-year-old Riley was the star hockey player for the Foghorns. They won the championship game! Riley's Emotions—Joy, Sadness, Anger, Fear, and Disgust—never stopped supporting their girl. They had helped her build a beautiful Sense of Self from her beliefs and memories. It said, *"I'm a good person."*

Riley was invited to a hockey camp. It was run by the coach from Riley's future high school team, the Fire Hawks. Riley remembered **past mistakes** she'd made and wondered if she'd be good enough for the team.

But Joy wasn't worried at all. Any bad memory that made Riley upset went straight to the **Back of the Mind**.

Joy and Sadness brought Riley's good memory of winning the game to the **Belief System**, where Riley's beliefs formed. The new belief that grew from the memory made Riley's **Sense of Self** glow even brighter.

Later that night, an alarm went off in Headquarters. *Beep! Beeep!*

Suddenly, **Mind Workers** appeared. They **tore apart** the console and made a few updates. After all, Riley was a teenager now. It was time for some **big changes**!

The Emotions tried out the new console, but every time they pushed a button, Riley **overreacted**. First, she **snapped** at her mother. Then she **cried** about snapping at her mother! Was the console broken? The Emotions were afraid to use it.

Soon Riley was off to hockey camp with her friends Bree and Grace. But they had **bad news**: they'd been assigned to a different high school. Oh, no! What would Riley do without them next year?

Then Riley bumped into **Valentina Ortiz**, the Fire Hawks' captain. *Gulp!* Val was her hockey hero.

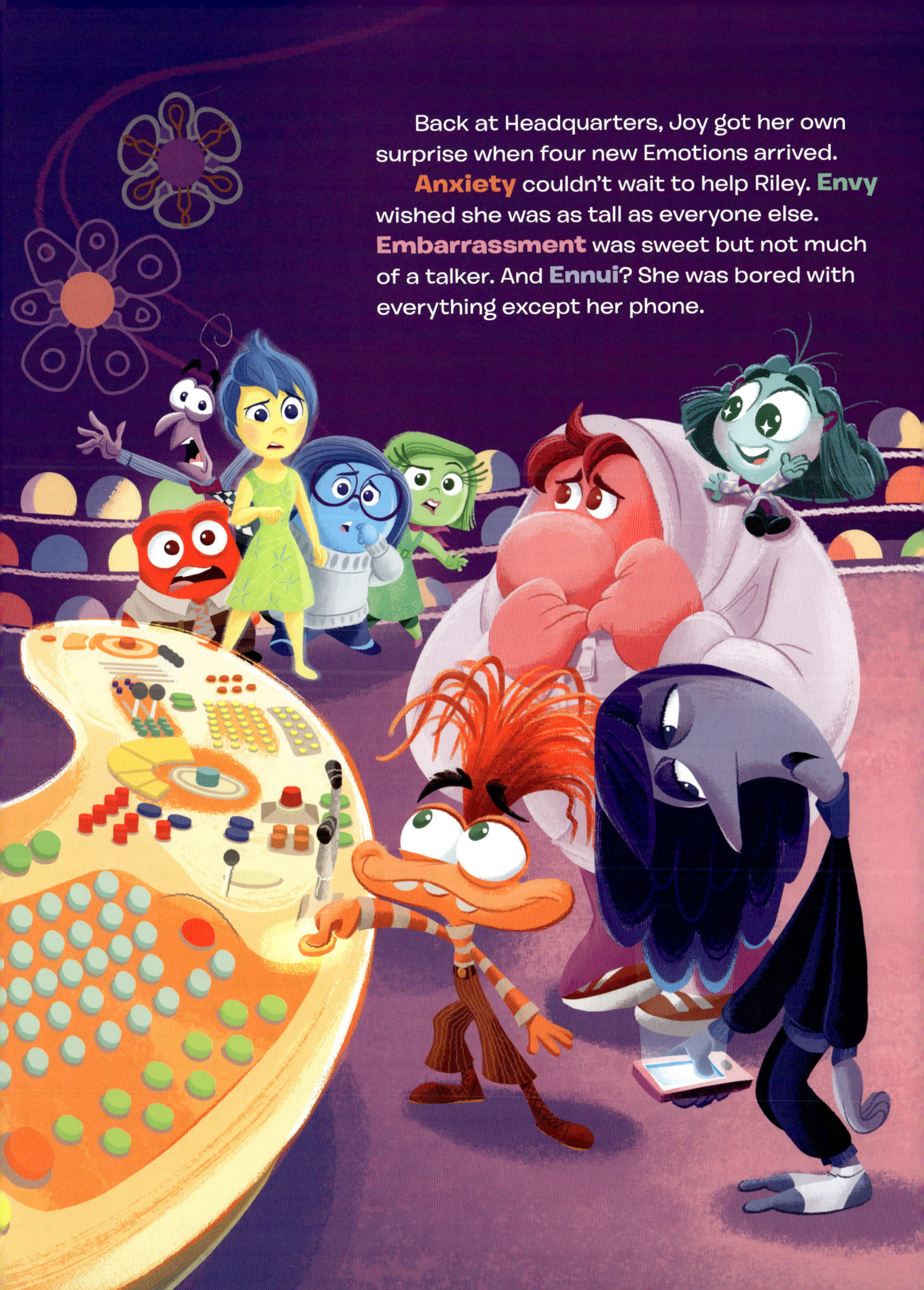

Back at Headquarters, Joy got her own surprise when four new Emotions arrived. **Anxiety** couldn't wait to help Riley. **Envy** wished she was as tall as everyone else. **Embarrassment** was sweet but not much of a talker. And **Ennui**? She was bored with everything except her phone.

Anxiety was determined to get Riley onto the Fire Hawks team so she would have friends in high school. Joy thought Riley should **just have fun**. She inspired Riley to take silly selfies with Bree and Grace.

But the coach wanted them to focus. **She took away everyone's phones!** Riley was so embarrassed.

Anxiety was certain that Riley wouldn't make the team if she didn't change. She needed a newer and better Sense of Self to become a newer and better Riley. Anxiety **yanked the Sense of Self from its pedestal** and launched it to the Back of the Mind!

When Joy and the other Emotions protested, Anxiety sent them to the vault, where Riley's secrets were kept. Trapped inside, they met **Bloofy** and **Pouchy**, characters from a preschool TV show that Riley secretly still liked. **Lance Slashblade** was a video game hero that she had a crush on. And Riley's **Deep Dark Secret** was, well . . . you don't want to know.

Pouchy offered some items to help them escape.
Anger chose the **exploding dynamite**!

The Emotions had to hurry to the Back of the Mind to find Riley's old Sense of Self. But they needed some help from Headquarters. It was up to Sadness to **sneak in through the Recall Tube**!

The rest of the Emotions followed the Stream of Consciousness, which carried objects that Riley was thinking about. It would lead them to the Back of the Mind.

Along their journey, the Emotions discovered that Anxiety was ordering Mind Workers to imagine **everything that could go wrong** for Riley. Anxiety believed this would help prepare her for the final game at camp. But it made Riley super stressed!

So Joy started imagining things going right for Riley. One by one, the Mind Workers **joined her**! But then the Mind Police showed up! The Emotions escaped by soaring away on a giant balloon.

Anxiety needed a new plan—and ideas—to prepare Riley for the game. She started a **brainstorm**!

Ideas rained from the sky, pummeling the Emotions and their balloon. It was going to pop! Suddenly, **a big idea swooped by**. The Emotions leapt onto the idea and soared out of the storm!

Now Riley was ready for the game. She tried to look and act like a Fire Hawk. Grace and Bree **hardly knew their best friend anymore**.

Meanwhile, the Emotions finally reached the Back of the Mind. They discovered a **massive mountain** of all the bad memories Joy had thrown away. Riley's old Sense of Self was at the top!

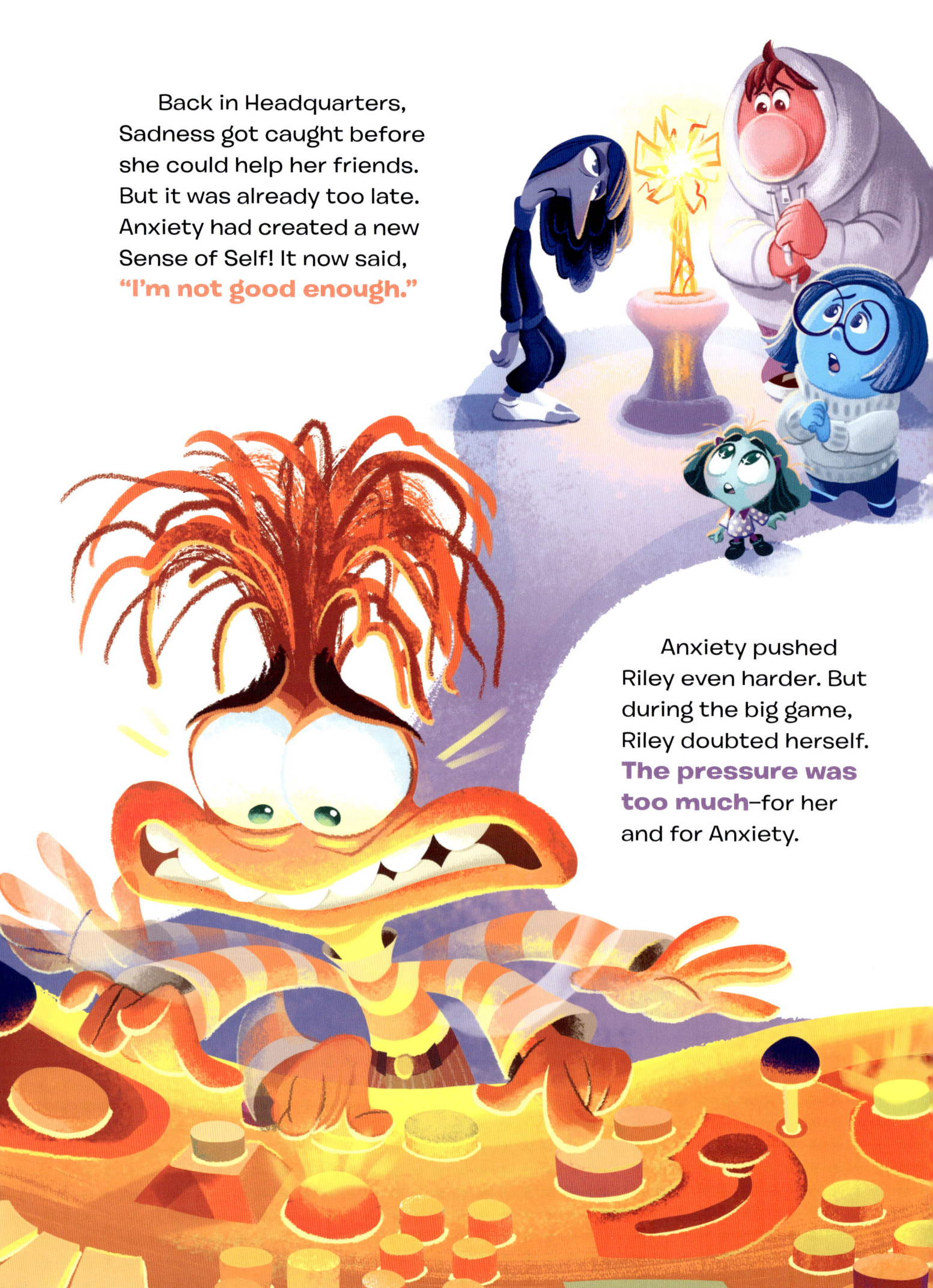

Back in Headquarters, Sadness got caught before she could help her friends. But it was already too late. Anxiety had created a new Sense of Self! It now said, **"I'm not good enough."**

Anxiety pushed Riley even harder. But during the big game, Riley doubted herself. **The pressure was too much**–for her and for Anxiety.

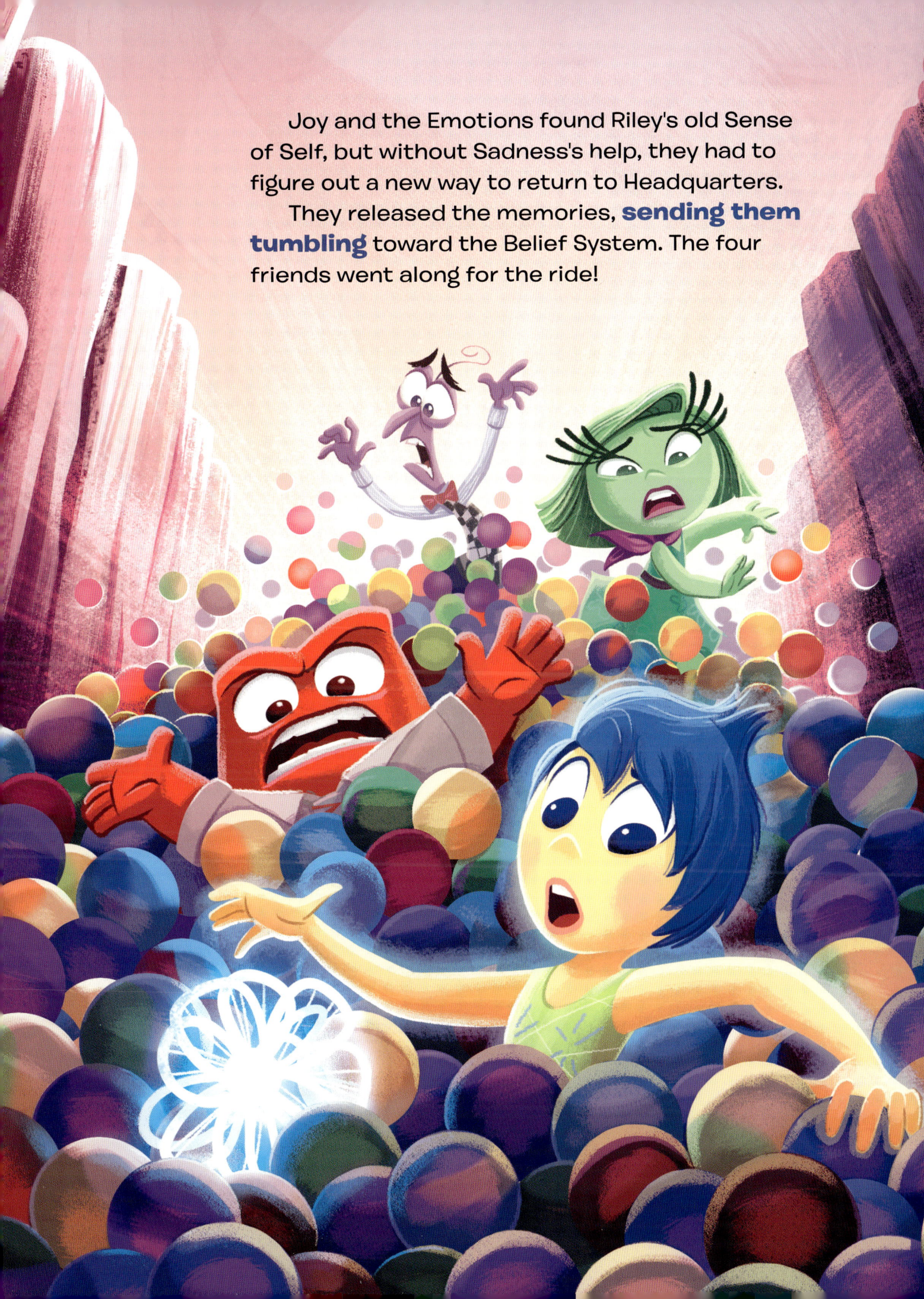

Joy and the Emotions found Riley's old Sense of Self, but without Sadness's help, they had to figure out a new way to return to Headquarters. They released the memories, **sending them tumbling** toward the Belief System. The four friends went along for the ride!

As the bad memories poured into the Belief System, new beliefs sprouted, creating a glow that was brighter than ever before! The beliefs began to form **Riley's true Sense of Self**—one that included the good, the bad, and everything in between.

Joy returned to Headquarters and **calmed Anxiety**. Riley began to relax, too. She finally knew what she needed to do.

Riley apologized to her friends. She'd been feeling uncertain about herself and the future. But her friends—both old and new—would be there to support her. **Riley wasn't alone.**

Even though Riley and her Sense of Self were still changing, the Emotions knew one thing: **they would always love their girl**.

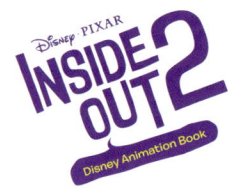

글 신시아 리우 | 그림 앨런 뱃슨 | 옮김 박혜원

1판 1쇄 펴낸 날 | 2024년 8월 10일

펴낸이 장영재
펴낸곳 (주)미르북컴퍼니
자회사 더모던
전 화 02)3141-4421
팩 스 0505-333-4428
등 록 2012년 3월 16일(제313-2012-81호)
주 소 서울시 마포구 성미산로32길 12, 2층 (우 03983)
e-mail sanhonjinju@naver.com
카 페 cafe.naver.com/mirbookcompany
인스타그램 www.instagram.com/mirbooks

ⓒ 2024 Disney/Pixar. all rights reserved.

이 책의 한국어판 저작권은 Disney/Pixar와 정식 계약 뒤 사용, 제작하고 있습니다.
저작권법에 의해 한국 내에서 보호받는 저작물이므로 무단 전재와 복제를 금합니다.

KC인증정보 **품명** 아동 도서 **사용연령** 4~7세 **제조년월일** 2024년 8월 10일 **제조국** 대한민국 **연락처** 02)3141-4421 서울시 마포구 성미산로32길 12, 2층 **주의사항** 종이에 베이거나 긁히지 않도록 조심하세요. 책 모서리가 날카로우니 던지거나 떨어뜨리지 마세요.